HIS

HOLINESS

THE DALAI LAMA

and

HOWARD C. CUTLER, M.D.

Riverhead Books

a member of Penguin Group (USA) Inc.

New York

2010

The
Essence
of Happiness

The

Essence

of Happiness

A Guidebook for Living

RIVERHEAD BOOKS

Published by the Penguin Group

Penguin Group (USA) Inc., 375 Hudson Street, New York, New York
10014, USA · Penguin Group (Canada), 90 Eglinton Avenue East, Suite 700, Toronto,
Ontario M4P 2Y3, Canada (a division of Pearson Penguin Canada Inc.) · Penguin Books
Ltd, 80 Strand, London WC2R 0RL, England · Penguin Ireland, 25 St Stephen's Green,
Dublin 2, Ireland (a division of Penguin Books Ltd) · Penguin Group (Australia),
250 Camberwell Road, Camberwell, Victoria 3124, Australia (a division of Pearson
Australia Group Pty Ltd) · Penguin Books India Pvt Ltd, 11 Community Centre,
Panchsheel Park, New Delhi–110 017, India · Penguin Group (NZ),
67 Apollo Drive, Rosedale, North Shore 0632, New Zealand (a division of
Pearson New Zealand Ltd) · Penguin Books (South Africa) (Pty) Ltd,
24 Sturdee Avenue, Rosebank, Johannesburg 2196, South Africa

Penguin Books Ltd, Registered Offices: 80 Strand, London WC2R 0RL, England

Library of Congress Cataloging-in-Publication Data

Bstan-'dzin-rgya-mtsho, Dalai Lama XIV, date.
The essence of happiness : a guidebook to living / His Holiness the Dalai Lama and
Howard C. Cutler.
p.   cm.
ISBN 978-1-59448-789-7
1. Religious life–Buddhism.   2. Happiness–Religious aspects–Buddhism.
3. Buddhism–Doctrines.   I. Cutler, Howard C.   II. Title.
III. Title: Guidebook to living.
BQ7935.B774E87   2010   2010032701
294.3'444–dc22

Printed in the United States of America
1   3   5   7   9   10   8   6   4   2

Book design by Claire Naylon Vaccaro

While the authors have made every effort to provide accurate telephone numbers and
Internet addresses at the time of publication, neither the publisher nor the authors
assume any responsibility for errors, or for changes that occur after publication.
Further, the publisher does not have any control over and does not assume any
responsibility for author or third-party websites or their content.

Contents

Foreword

The Essence of Happiness has been extracted from *The Art of Happiness: A Handbook for Living,* a book based on extensive conversations between His Holiness the Dalai Lama and Dr. Howard C. Cutler, a Western psychiatrist. Dr. Cutler's aim was to collaborate on a project that would present the Dalai Lama's views on leading a happier life, augmented by observations and commentary from his own Western perspective.

Dr. Cutler received his medical degree from the University of Arizona College of Medicine. He completed specialty training in psychiatry at the Good

Samaritan Medical Center in Phoenix, and is a diplomate of the American Board of Psychiatry and Neurology. Dr. Cutler currently resides in Phoenix, where he has a private psychiatric practice.

His Holiness Tenzin Gyatso, the fourteenth Dalai Lama, is the spiritual and temporal leader of the Tibetan people. In 1989 His Holiness was awarded the Nobel Peace Prize for his non-violent struggle for the liberation of Tibet. Since 1959 he has been living in exile in India. Tibet continues to be occupied by Communist China.

THE HIGH OFFICE OF TIBET
DHARAMSALA, INDIA

Introduction

In this book we have distilled the essential principles and practices of *The Art of Happiness: A Handbook for Living*, selecting key passages that encapsulate that book's fundamental concepts. To introduce this volume, I think it may be helpful to view it within the wider context of the Art of Happiness book series, beginning with a brief history.

The Art of Happiness was published in 1998, and despite a small first printing and modest expectations of success, it quickly became an international bestseller, with readers eventually in the millions. After the book's release, I found myself still wishing to explore the subject of happiness with the Dalai Lama, in greater depth. Although we had covered the key principles, I felt there was still much to learn, recalling many past conversations in which he had reminded me, "Although achieving genuine happiness is possible, it is not a simple matter. There are many levels. . . . You need a variety of approaches. . . . The more sophisticated your level of education and knowledge about what truly leads to happiness, the more effective you will be in achieving it."

So when a convergence of events created the opportunity to continue our meetings, I was delighted. These discussions evolved into an ongoing collaboration on a series of books, including *The Art of Happiness at Work* (2003) and *The Art of Happiness in a Troubled World* (2009). Two more volumes are currently planned to complete the series.

This brings us to *The Essence of Happiness*. As I have just suggested a rationale for expanding the original volume into a series, the idea of condensing or abridging the same book may seem contradictory. But there is no conflict. There are many approaches to happiness, each useful under different circumstances. And sometimes, all we need are a few simple reminders of fundamental truths.

How can this book be useful? First, for those who are uncertain about which attitudes or behaviors lead to genuine happiness, it can help navigate a true course toward happiness–with an approach supported by 2,500 years of empirical testing by countless Buddhist practitioners and, more recently, by scientific verification. Second, for those who do know the true path to happiness, but who get so caught up in the grind of daily life that they forget these basic inner truths and veer off course, these nuggets of wisdom can act as *reminders* to help get them back on track. And for those who clearly remember these principles but fail to act on them, this book can encourage them to apply the principles in their daily lives, inspired by a man who has found genuine peace and happiness by following this path himself.

Because the structure and format of this book depart slightly from the customary format of the

Art of Happiness series, before closing I'd like to add a few comments about the editing of this book.

The Art of Happiness is divided into five main parts, then subdivided into chapters. *The Essence of Happiness* follows the same five-part structure, and within each part are excerpts related to the main themes found in the corresponding part of *The Art of Happiness*. These excerpts were extracted from *The Art of Happiness*, then loosely grouped by theme and reorganized, without reference to their original location. Therefore, the sequence of excerpts does not necessarily follow the same order of the chapters in the earlier book. Also, when extracting the excerpts, occasionally I found it necessary to do some minor editing, either for grammar or to preserve the clarity and correct meaning of a passage, once it was taken out of the context of the wider discussion. In a few cases, I also edited for conciseness, although generally I felt it more important to keep the Dalai Lama's words as they appeared in the original dialogues; I took greater liberties in editing portions of my own commentary.

Finally, in the tenth-anniversary edition of *The Art of Happiness*, the Dalai Lama writes, "Our aim has been to share with others the conviction that there is a lot each of us can do to achieve greater happiness in our lives and, more important, to draw attention to the tremendous inner resources that are at the disposal of each of us." I hope that this volume fulfills those same objectives and that you will find something of practical value in these pages, to help you achieve genuine and lasting happiness.

I.

The Purpose of Life

I believe that the very purpose of our life
is to seek happiness. That is clear.
Whether one believes in religion or not,
whether one believes in this religion
or that religion, we all are seeking
something better in life. So, I think,
the very motion of our life is
toward happiness.

Our days are numbered. At this very moment, many thousands are born into the world—some destined to live only a few days or weeks, others destined to push through to the century mark, perhaps even a bit beyond, savoring every taste life has to offer: triumph, despair, joy, hatred, and love. We never know. But whether we live a day or a century, a central question always remains: What is the purpose of our life? What makes our lives meaningful? · H.C.

The purpose of our life needs to be
positive. We weren't born with the
purpose of causing trouble, harming
others. For our life to be of value, I
think we must develop basic good
human qualities—warmth, kindness,
compassion. Then our life becomes
meaningful and more peaceful—happier.

In Buddhism, the principle of causality
is accepted as a natural law — if you want
a particular event or experience to occur,
then the logical thing to do is to seek
the causes and conditions that give
rise to it. . . . So, if you desire happiness,
you should seek the causes that give
rise to it, and if you don't desire
suffering, then what you should do is

ensure that the causes and conditions
that would give rise to it no longer
arise.

The purpose of our life is happiness. That simple statement can be used as a powerful tool in helping us navigate through life's daily problems. From that perspective, our task becomes one of discarding the things that lead to suffering and accumulating the things that lead to happiness. The method, the daily practice, involves gradually increasing our awareness and understanding of what truly leads to happiness and what doesn't. · H.C.

Although it is possible to achieve happiness, happiness is not a simple thing. There are many levels. In Buddhism, for instance, there is a reference to the four factors of fulfillment, or happiness: wealth, worldly satisfaction, spirituality, and enlightenment. Together they embrace the totality of an individual's quest for happiness.

When life becomes too complicated, overwhelming,

or confusing, it's useful to stand back and remind

ourselves of our overall purpose or goal. Take an

hour, an afternoon, or even several days to reflect on

what it is that will truly bring us happiness, and then

reset our priorities based on that. This can put our

life back in proper context, allow a fresh perspective,

and enable us to see what direction to take. . . . The

turning toward happiness as a valid goal and the

conscious decision to systematically seek it can

profoundly change the rest of our lives. · H.C.

If we utilize our favorable circumstances, such as our good health or wealth, in positive ways, in helping others, they can be contributory factors in achieving a happier life. And of course we enjoy these things — our material facilities, success, and so on. But without the right mental attitude, without attention to the mental factor, these things have very little impact on our long-term feelings of happiness.

If you harbor hateful thoughts or intense anger deep within yourself, it ruins your health; thus it destroys one of the factors conventionally considered necessary for a happy life. . . . Or, even if you have wonderful possessions, in an intense moment of anger you may feel like throwing or breaking them, they mean nothing, so there is no guarantee that wealth alone can give you the joy or fulfillment you are seeking. . . . These examples indicate the tremendous influence that the mental state, the mind factor, has on our experience of daily life. Naturally, then, we have to take that factor very seriously.

Now sometimes people confuse
happiness with pleasure. . . . True
happiness relates more to the mind and
heart. Happiness that depends mainly on
physical pleasure is unstable: one day it's
there, the next day it may not be.

Sometimes, making the "right choice" in life is difficult because it involves some sacrifice of our momentary pleasures. . . . But framing any decision we face with the question "Will this bring me happiness?" can be a powerful strategy to help us skillfully conduct all areas of our lives, not just in the decision whether to indulge in drugs or that third piece of banana cream pie. Asking ourselves this fundamental question puts a new slant on things, shifting the focus from what we are denying ourselves to what we are truly seeking—ultimate happiness. · H.C.

"Are you happy?" I asked the Dalai Lama.

"Yes," he said. He paused, then added, "Yes. . . . Definitely." There was a quiet sincerity in his voice that left no doubt.

"But is happiness a reasonable goal for most of us? Is it really possible?"

"Yes," he replied, "I believe that happiness can be achieved through training the mind." · H.C.

When I say "training the mind" in this
context I'm not referring to "mind"
merely as one's cognitive ability or
intellect. Rather, I'm using the term in
the sense of the Tibetan word *sem,* which
has a much broader meaning, closer to
"psyche" or "spirit": it includes intellect
and feeling, heart and mind. By bringing
about a certain inner discipline, we can

undergo a transformation of our attitude,

our entire outlook and approach to

living.

The concept of achieving true happiness has, in the West, always seemed ill-defined, elusive, ungraspable. Even the word "happy" is derived from the Icelandic word happ, *meaning luck or chance. . . . It didn't seem the sort of thing that could be developed simply by "training the mind"—an idea that has been the cornerstone of Buddhist practice for 2,500 years. Recently, however, with new scientific research consistently supporting the Dalai Lama's views, we've seen Buddhist principles con-*

verging with Western science, as researchers now

agree that happiness can be deliberately cultivated,

much like learning any other skill. · H.C.

The greater the level of calmness of our mind, the greater our peace of mind, the greater our ability to enjoy a happy and joyful life.

When we speak of a calm state of mind or peace of mind, we shouldn't confuse that with a totally insensitive, apathetic state of mind. Having a calm or peaceful state of mind doesn't mean being totally spaced out or completely empty. Peace of mind or a calm state of mind is rooted in affection and compassion. There is a very high level of sensitivity and feeling there.

As long as there is a lack of the inner
discipline that brings calmness of mind,
no matter what external facilities or
conditions you have, they will never give
you the feeling of joy and happiness
that you are seeking. On the other hand,
if you possess this inner quality, a
calmness of mind, a degree of stability
within, then even if you lack
various external facilities that you

would normally consider necessary for happiness, it is still possible to live a happy and joyful life.

We don't need more money, we don't need greater success or fame, we don't need the perfect body or even the perfect mate—right now, at this very moment, we have a mind, which is all the basic equipment we need to achieve complete happiness. · H.C.

It is felt that a disciplined mind leads to happiness and an undisciplined mind leads to suffering, and in fact it is said that bringing about discipline within one's mind is the essence of the Buddha's teaching. . . . Here, I'm referring to self-discipline, not discipline that's externally imposed on you by someone else. Also, I'm referring to discipline that's applied to overcome your negative qualities. A criminal

gang may need discipline to perform

a successful robbery, but that discipline

is useless.

When we speak of this inner discipline, it can of course involve many things, many methods. But generally speaking, one begins by identifying those factors that lead to happiness and those factors that lead to suffering. Having done this, one then sets about gradually eliminating those mental factors, emotions, or behaviors that lead to suffering and cultivating those that lead to happiness. That is the way.

Achieving genuine happiness may require a transformation of your outlook, your way of thinking, and this is not a simple matter. You shouldn't have the notion that there is just one key, a secret, and if you can get that right, then everything will be okay. It is similar to taking proper care of the physical body; you need a variety of vitamins and nutrients, not just one or two. In the same way, in

order to achieve happiness, you need a
variety of approaches and methods to
deal with and overcome the varied and
complex negative mental states.

The first step in seeking happiness is learning. We first have to learn how negative emotions and behaviors are harmful, not only to one personally, but harmful to society and the future of the whole world as well. This enhances our determination to face and overcome them. Then there is the realization of the beneficial aspects of the positive emotions and behaviors. Once we realize that, we become determined to cherish,

develop, and increase those positive

emotions no matter how difficult that is.

There is a kind of spontaneous

willingness from within.

Survey after survey has shown that it is unhappy people who tend to be most self-focused and are often socially withdrawn, brooding, and even antagonistic. . . . In contrast, studies show that happy people are more likely to attract a mate and have stronger marriages and better relationships in general. They enjoy better physical health, living up to ten years longer. Happiness also leads to better mental health, greater creativity, resilience, and an increased capacity to deal with adversity. In addition, happy individuals achieve greater career success and earn higher incomes, essentially enjoying greater personal success on every level. . . . And, most important, they are found to be more loving and forgiving than unhappy people, more willing to reach out and help others. · H.C.

Transforming your mind takes time.
There are a lot of negative mental traits,
so you need to address and counteract
each one of these. That isn't easy. It
requires the repeated application of
various techniques and taking the time to
familiarize yourself with the practices.
It's a process of learning.

No matter what activity or practice we
are pursuing, there isn't anything that
isn't made easier through constant
familiarity and training. Through
training, we can change; we can
transform ourselves.

The cultivation of greater happiness by training the mind is possible because of the very structure and function of the brain. Although genetically hardwired with certain innate or instinctual behavior patterns, the brain is not static, not irrevocably fixed. It is adaptable, malleable, changing individual neurons and reconfiguring its wiring according to new thoughts and experiences. The brain's inherent capacity to change in response to learning is known as "neuroplasticity"—a process that provides the physiological basis for the idea of

training the mind for happiness and the possibil-

ity of inner transformation. · H.C.

At the beginning, the implementation of the positive practices is very small, so the negative influences are still very powerful. However, eventually, as you gradually build up the positive practices, the negative behaviors are automatically diminished. . . . Through repeated practice of these methods we can get to the point where some disturbance may occur but the negative effects on our mind remain on the surface, like the waves that may ripple on the surface of an ocean but don't have much effect deep down.

You should never lose sight of the importance of having a realistic attitude — of being very sensitive to and respectful of the concrete reality of your situation as you proceed on the path toward your ultimate goal. Recognize the difficulties inherent in your path, and the fact that it may take time and a consistent effort. It's also important to make a clear distinction in your mind

between your *ideals* and the *standards*

by which you judge your progress.

Change takes time.

Every day, as soon as you get up, you can develop a sincere positive motivation, thinking, "I will utilize this day in a more positive way. I should not waste this very day." And then, at night before bed, check what you've done, asking yourself, "Did I utilize this day as I planned?"

The demarcation between a positive and a negative desire or action is not whether it gives you an immediate feeling of satisfaction but whether it ultimately results in positive or negative consequences.

Certain desires are positive: a desire for
happiness, for peace, for a friendlier
world. These are very useful. But at
some point, desires can become
unreasonable. . . . Greed is an exaggerated
form of desire, and that leads to trouble.
Although the underlying motive of greed
is to seek satisfaction, the irony is that
even after obtaining the object of your
desire, you are still not satisfied. *The true*

antidote to greed is contentment. If you have a strong sense of contentment, it doesn't matter whether you obtain the object or not; either way, you are still content.

Our feelings of contentment are strongly influenced by our tendency to compare. . . . Constant comparison with those who are smarter, more beautiful, or more successful than we are also tends to breed envy, frustration, and unhappiness. But we can use this same principle in a positive way; we can increase our feeling of life satisfaction by comparing ourselves with those who are less fortunate than we are and by reflecting on all the things we have. . . .

So, how can we achieve inner contentment?

There are two methods. One method is to obtain everything that we want and desire—all the money, houses, cars, the perfect mate and the perfect body. The Dalai Lama has pointed out the disadvantage of this approach—if our wants and desires remain unchecked, sooner or later we will run up against something that we want but can't have. The second method is not to have what we want, but rather to want what we have. H.C.

Proper utilization of time is so important. While we have this body, and especially this amazing human brain, I think every minute is something precious. Our day-to-day existence is very much alive with hope, although there is no guarantee of our future. There is no guarantee that tomorrow at this time we will be here. But still we are working for that purely on the basis of hope. So, we

need to make the best use of our time. I
believe that the proper utilization of time
is this: if you can, serve other people,
other sentient beings. If not, at least
refrain from harming them. I think that
is the whole basis of my philosophy.

A stunning recent study has found that happiness is highly contagious, spreading in social networks just like a virus. Other studies show that positive emotions act as an antidote to prejudice, causing changes in the brain that prevent the instinctual bias against those we perceive as different, breaking down the barriers between Us and Them! Investigators have also linked higher levels of happiness with greater freedom and democracy in a nation! So, it could be argued that if you are truly concerned about building a better world, it is your duty to be happy. · H.C.

I have often witnessed how the Dalai Lama's personal happiness seems to manifest as a simple willingness to reach out to others, creating a feeling of affinity and spreading goodwill, even in the briefest of encounters.

One morning the Dalai Lama was walking back to his hotel room. Noticing one of the housekeeping staff by the elevators, he stopped to ask, "Where are you from?" For a moment she appeared taken aback by this man in strange maroon robes and his entourage, but she smiled and answered shyly, "Mexico." They briefly chatted before he walked on, leaving her looking excited and pleased. The next morning, she appeared at the same spot with another housekeeper, and they greeted him warmly as he got into the elevator. The interaction was brief, but they both seemed to be flushed with happiness as they returned to work. Every day after that, they were joined by a few more of the housekeeping staff at the designated time and place, until by the end of the week there were dozens of maids in their crisp *gray and white uniforms forming a receiving line*

that stretched along the length of the path that led

to the elevators. · H.C.

II.

Human Warmth and Compassion

If you want others to be happy, practice
compassion; and if you want yourself to
be happy, practice compassion.

There is no question that happiness brings tremendous personal rewards. But it is also critical to point out that cultivating greater happiness benefits not only oneself, but also one's family, community, and society. *This is one of the key principles underlying* The Art of Happiness. · H.C.

Now, we are made to seek happiness.
And it is clear that feelings of love,
affection, closeness, and compassion
bring happiness. I believe that every one
of us has the basis to be happy, to access
the warm and compassionate states of
mind that bring happiness.

In one of my favorite experiments, neuroscientist
Dr. Richard Davidson asked a Buddhist monk to
meditate intensively on compassion while he moni-
tored the monk's brain function in the lab. Brain
scans showed a dramatic increase in activity in the
monk's left prefrontal cortex as he deliberately
generated a compassionate state of mind—lighting
up the region of the brain associated with feel-
ings of happiness. . . . In another study, subjects
performed five "random acts of kindness" once a

week for six weeks. This resulted in a signifi-

cant increase in their levels of happiness and life

satisfaction. · H.C.

Within all beings there is the seed of perfection. However, compassion is required in order to activate that seed that is inherent in our hearts and minds.

I would regard a compassionate, warm,
kindhearted person as healthy. If you
maintain a feeling of compassion, loving-
kindness, then something automatically
opens your inner door. Through that,
you can communicate much more easily
with other people. And that feeling of
warmth creates a kind of openness.
You'll find that all human beings are just
like you, so you'll be able to relate to

them more easily. . . . Approaching others with the thought of compassion automatically changes your attitude toward them, reducing fear, self-doubt, and insecurity.

I think that there is often a danger of
confusing compassion with attachment.
So when we discuss compassion, we
must first make a distinction between
two types of love or compassion. One
kind of compassion is tinged with
attachment—the feeling of controlling
someone, or loving someone so that
person will love you back. This ordinary
type of love or compassion is quite

partial and biased. It is based on your mental projection, on your perceiving that person as a friend or loved one. And a relationship based on that alone is unstable.

But there is a second type of compassion that is free from such attachment. That is genuine compassion. That kind of compassion isn't so much based on the fact that this person or that person is dear to me. Rather, genuine compassion is based on the rationale that all human beings have an innate desire to be happy and overcome suffering, just like myself. And, just like myself, they have the natural right to fulfill this fundamental aspiration. With this as a foundation, you can feel compassion regardless of whether you view the other person as a friend or an enemy.

Compassion can be roughly defined in terms of a state of mind that is non-violent, non-harming, and non-aggressive. It is a mental attitude based on the wish for others to be free of their suffering and is associated with a sense of commitment, responsibility, and respect toward the other.

The Tibetan word for compassion, *tse-wa*,
refers to an attitude or state of mind that
includes not only a wish for the welfare of
others, a wish for others to be free of
their suffering, but also a wish for good
things for oneself.

In developing compassion, perhaps one could begin with the wish that one be free of suffering, and then take that natural feeling toward oneself and cultivate it, enhance it, and extend it out to include and embrace others.

If you wish to develop a feeling of
affinity or connectedness with others, a
feeling of openness, without fear or
apprehension, then my basic belief is
that you first need to realize the
usefulness of compassion. That's the key
factor. Once you accept the fact that
compassion is not something childish or
sentimental, once you realize that it is
something really worthwhile, realize its

deeper value, then you immediately

develop an attraction toward it, a

willingness to cultivate it.

Compassion isn't just a religious matter, it's an indispensable factor in day-to-day life, beginning at birth. Our very first act after birth is to suck our mother's milk. That's an act of affection, of compassion. Without that, we cannot survive. Then, our physical structure seems to be more suited to feelings of love, compassion, and affection; these are emotions that have beneficial effects on our physical health and emotional well-being. These gentler emotions and behaviors also lead to a happier family and community life.

There is a basic human level where
distinctions between people—gender,
race, religion, culture, and language—
break down. At this fundamental level,
we are all the same; each one of us
aspires to happiness and does not wish
to suffer. . . . Of course, there may be
differences in our cultural background,
way of life, our faith or color, but we are
all human beings, consisting of a human

body, human mind, and emotions. Wherever I meet people, I have the feeling that I am encountering another human being, just like myself. . . . If we can relate to others on that basic level and leave the differences aside, I think we can easily communicate, exchange ideas, and share experiences.

Can we cultivate ourselves to be more compassionate? If so, how do we do it? Here, I believe that profound recognition of the fundamental sameness of the human family and the deeply inter-connected nature of our well-being are crucially important. . . . I believe that as a species we need to ground our interaction with fellow human beings on recognition of these profound yet simple truths.

In generating compassion, you start by recognizing that you do not want suffering and that you have a right to have happiness. This can be verified or validated by your own experience. You then recognize that other people, just like yourself, also do not want to suffer and that they have a right to have happiness. So this becomes the basis of your beginning to generate compassion.

In one sense, one could define
compassion as the feeling of
unbearableness at the sight of other
people's suffering, other sentient beings'
suffering. And in order to generate that
feeling, one must first have an
appreciation of the seriousness or
intensity of another's suffering. So,
I think that the more fully one
understands suffering, and the various

kinds of suffering that we are subject to, the deeper will be one's level of compassion.

When you think about your own
suffering, you might feel overwhelmed,
helpless. There's a sense of being
burdened, a kind of dullness or
numbness. Now, in generating
compassion, when you're taking on
another's suffering, you may also
initially experience a certain discomfort,
a sense of unbearableness. But with
compassion, the feeling is much

different; underlying the uncomfortable feeling is a high level of alertness and determination because you are voluntarily and deliberately sharing another's suffering for a higher purpose. There's a feeling of connectedness and commitment, a willingness to reach out to others, a feeling of freshness rather than dullness.

In looking at the various means of developing compassion, I think that empathy is an important factor, the ability to appreciate another's suffering. . . . One can attempt to increase compassion by trying to empathize with another's feelings or experience, by using your imagination, your creativity, to visualize yourself in another's situation.

Whenever I meet people I always
approach them from the standpoint of
the most basic things we have in
common. We each have a physical
structure, a mind, emotions. We are all
born in the same way, and we all die. All
of us want happiness and do not want
to suffer. Looking at others from this
standpoint rather than emphasizing
secondary differences, such as the fact

that I am Tibetan, or a different color or religion, or have a different cultural background, allows me to have a feeling that I'm meeting someone just the same as me. I find that relating to others on that level makes it much easier to exchange and communicate with one another.

I think that empathy is important not only as a means of enhancing compassion, but I think that generally speaking, when dealing with others on any level, if you're having some difficulties, it's extremely helpful to be able to try to put yourself in the other person's place and see how you would react to the situation.

On a personal level, being open and sharing things can be very useful. Because of this nature, I can make friends more easily, and it's a matter not just of knowing people and having a superficial exchange but of really sharing my deepest problems and suffering. And it's the same thing when I hear good news; I immediately share it with others. So, I feel a sense of intimacy and connection with my friends.

I think that if one is seeking to build a truly satisfying relationship, the best way of bringing this about is to get to know the deeper nature of the person and relate to her or him on that level, instead of merely on the basis of superficial characteristics. And in this type of relationship there is a role for genuine compassion.

If you are running into relationship problems, it's often very helpful to simply stand back and reflect on the underlying nature and basis of that relationship. For example, among friendships there can be some that are based on wealth, power, or position. These friendships will continue as long as your wealth, power, or position is sustained, but the friendship will begin to disappear once those grounds are no longer there. On the other hand, there can be another kind of friendship based on true human feeling, a feeling of closeness, in which there is a sense of sharing and connectedness.

The factor that sustains a genuine

friendship is a feeling of affection.

Some relationships are based on sexual attraction. But there can be two principal types of sexual attraction-based relationships: the first type is based on pure sexual desire. A relationship built primarily on sexual desire is like a house built on a foundation of ice—as soon as the ice melts, the building collapses. In the second type, in addition to physical attraction there is an underlying appreciation of the value of the other person, a mutual respect, based on taking enough time to genuinely get to know each other's basic characteristics. This relationship will be much more long-lasting and reliable.

I think that, leaving aside how the
endless pursuit of romantic love may
affect our deeper spiritual growth, even
from the perspective of a conventional
way of life, the idealization of this
romantic love can be seen as an extreme.
Unlike those relationships based on
caring and genuine affection, this is
another matter. . . . It's something that
is based on fantasy, unattainable, and

therefore may be a source of frustration.
So, on that basis it cannot be seen as a
positive thing.

I think that in many cases people tend to
expect the other person to respond to
them in a positive way first, rather than
taking the initiative themselves to create
that possibility. I feel that's wrong; it
leads to problems and can act as a barrier
that just serves to promote a feeling of
isolation from others. So, if you wish to
overcome that feeling of isolation and
loneliness, I think that your underlying

attitude makes a tremendous difference.
And approaching others with the thought
of compassion in your mind is the best
way to do this.

It is one of my fundamental beliefs
that not only do we inherently possess
the potential for compassion, but I
believe that the basic or underlying
nature of human beings is gentle
and compassionate. . . . That is the
predominant feature of human nature.
However, I feel it is not enough that this
is our underlying nature — *we must also
develop a deep awareness and appreciation*

of that fact, changing how we perceive ourselves. This can have a very real impact on how we interact with others and how we conduct our daily lives.

Once we conclude that the basic nature of human-

ity is compassionate rather than aggressive, our

relationship to the world around us changes im-

mediately. Seeing others as basically compassion-

ate instead of hostile and selfish helps us relax,

trust, live at ease. It makes us happier. ˙ H.C.

When human intelligence and human
goodness or affection are used together,
all human actions become constructive.
When we combine a warm heart with
knowledge and education, we can learn to
respect others' views and others' rights.
This becomes the basis of a spirit of
reconciliation that can be used to
overcome aggression and resolve our
conflict. So, no matter how much

violence or how many bad things we have to go through, I believe that the ultimate solution to our conflicts, both internal and external, lies in returning to our basic or underlying human nature, which is gentle and compassionate.

III.

Transforming
Suffering

Problems are bound to arise in life. Trying to avoid or simply not think about them may provide temporary relief, but there is a better approach: if you're in a battle, as long as you remain ignorant of the status and combat capability of your enemy, you will be totally unprepared and paralyzed by fear. But if you know your opponents' fighting capability, weaponry, and so on, then you're in a much better position

when you engage in the war. Similarly,

directly confronting your suffering rather

than avoiding it will help you appreciate

the depth and nature of the problem,

and you'll be in a better position to deal

with it.

As long as we view suffering as an unnatural state, an abnormal condition that we fear, avoid, and reject, we will never uproot the causes of suffering and begin to live a happier life. · H.C.

Our attitude toward suffering becomes very important because it can affect how we cope with suffering when it arises. Now, our usual attitude consists of an intense aversion and intolerance of our pain and suffering. However, if we can transform our attitude toward suffering, adopt an attitude that allows us greater tolerance of it, then this can do much to help counteract feelings of mental unhappiness, dissatisfaction, and discontent.

While it is natural to recoil from suffering, some-times it can strengthen us, even bring out our best. As a character in Graham Greene's The Third Man *observes, "In Italy for thirty years under the Borgias, they had warfare, terror, murder, and bloodshed—but they produced Michelangelo, Leonardo da Vinci, and the Renaissance. In Swit-zerland, they have brotherly love, five hundred years of democracy and peace, and what did they produce? The cuckoo clock."*

At other times suffering can soften us, causing a vulnerability that can deepen our connection with others—as poet William Wordsworth said, "A deep distress hath humanized my soul." · H.C.

In searching for some meaning or
practical value of suffering, there is one
aspect of our suffering that is of vital
importance: awareness of your pain and
suffering helps you develop your capacity
for empathy, the capacity that allows
you to relate to others' feelings and
suffering. This enhances your capacity
for compassion toward others. So, as an
aid in helping us connect with others, it

can be seen as having value. Looking at suffering in this way, our attitude may begin to change—our suffering may not be as bad as we think.

The time and effort we spend searching for meaning in suffering will pay great rewards when bad things begin to strike. But in order to reap those rewards, we must begin our search for meaning when things are going well. A tree with strong roots can withstand the most violent storm, but the tree can't grow roots just as the storm appears on the horizon. · H.C.

Reflecting on suffering has tremendous importance because by realizing the nature of suffering, you will develop greater resolve to put an end to the causes of suffering and the unwholesome deeds that lead to suffering. And it will increase your enthusiasm for engaging in the wholesome actions and deeds that lead to happiness and joy.

The point that has to be borne in mind
is that the reason why reflection on
suffering is so important is that there is
a possibility of a way out; there is an
alternative. *There is a possibility of freedom
from suffering.*

There are many ways in which we actively contribute to our own experience of mental unrest and suffering. Although, in general, afflictive emotions can come naturally, often it is our own reinforcement of those negative emotions that makes things so much worse. For instance, when we have anger or hatred toward a person, if we think about the injustices done to us, the ways that we have been unfairly treated, and keep

thinking about it over and over, it feeds

the hatred. Through this constant

familiarity and thinking, we ourselves

can make our emotions more intense and

powerful.

We often add to our pain and suffering by being overly sensitive, overreacting to minor things, and sometimes taking things too personally. We tend to take small things too seriously and blow them up out of proportion, while at the same time we often remain indifferent to the really important things, those things that have profound effects on our lives and long-term consequences and implications. So I think that to a large extent, whether or not you suffer depends on how you *respond* to a given situation.

The beginning of being released from suffering is to investigate one of the primary causes: resistance to change. · H.C.

It's extremely important to investigate
the causes or origins of suffering, how it
arises. One must begin that process by
appreciating the impermanent, transient
nature of our existence. All things,
events, and phenomena are dynamic,
changing every moment; nothing remains
static. . . . So, at any given moment, no
matter how pleasant or pleasurable your
experience may be, it will not last. This

becomes the basis of a category of suffering known in Buddhism as the "suffering of change."

The act of acceptance, of acknowledging that change is a natural part of our interactions with others, can play a vital role in our relationships. We may discover that it is at the very time when we may feel most disappointed, as if something has gone out of the relationship, that a profound transformation can occur. · H.C.

Although you may not always be able to
avoid difficult situations, you can modify
the extent to which you suffer by how
you choose to respond to the situation.

Each of us has done some wrong. There are things we regret—things we have done, things we should have done, or things we didn't do. Acknowledging our wrongdoings with a genuine sense of remorse can help keep us on the right track, encouraging us to rectify our mistakes and correct things in the future. But if we allow regret to degenerate into guilt, holding on to the memory of our past transgressions with self-blame and self-hatred, this serves no purpose other than becoming a relentless source of self-punishment and self-induced suffering. · H.C.

The ability to look at events from
different perspectives can be very helpful.
Then, practicing this, one can use certain
experiences, certain tragedies, to develop
a calmness of mind. One must realize
that every phenomenon, every event, has
different aspects. Everything is of a
relative nature.

In our daily life, problems invariably arise. But problems themselves do not automatically cause suffering. If we can directly address our problem and focus our energies on finding a solution, for instance, the problem can be transformed into a challenge. · H.C.

Generally speaking, once you're already
in a difficult situation, it isn't possible to
change your attitude simply by adopting
a particular thought once or twice.
Rather, it's a process of learning, training,
and getting used to new viewpoints that
enables you to deal with the difficulty.

A supple mind, a flexible mode of thinking, helps us address our problems from a variety of perspectives. And conversely, deliberately examining problems "from different angles" is a kind of flexibility training for the mind. . . . Life today is characterized by sudden, unexpected, and sometimes violent change. A supple mind can help us reconcile the changes going on all around us. Without cultivating a pliant mind, our outlook becomes brittle and our relationship to the world becomes characterized by fear. But by adopting a flexible approach to life, we can maintain our com-

posure even under the most turbulent conditions.

It is through our efforts to achieve a flexible mind

that we can nurture the resilience of the human

spirit. · H.C.

It seems that whenever there are intense
emotions involved, there tends to be a
disparity between how things appear and
how they really are.

In general, if we carefully examine any given situation in an unbiased and honest way, we'll realize that to a large extent we are also responsible for the unfolding of events. . . . This practice involves looking at things in a holistic way—realizing that there are many events contributing to a situation.

Whether we are successful or not, even the honest attempt to search for our own contribution to a problem allows a certain shift of focus that helps to break through the narrow patterns of thinking that lead to the destructive feeling of unfairness that is the source of so much discontent in ourselves and in the world.

A balanced and skillful approach to life, taking care to avoid extremes, becomes a very important factor in conducting one's everyday existence. It is important in all aspects of life.

Once there was a disciple of a Greek philosopher

who was commanded by his Master for three years

to give money to everyone who insulted him. When

this period was over, the Master said, "Now you

can go to Athens and learn Wisdom." Upon enter-

ing Athens, the disciple met a certain wise man

sitting at the gate, insulting everybody who came

and went. He also insulted the disciple, who burst

out laughing. "Why do you laugh?" asked the

wise man. "Because," said the disciple, "for three

years I have been paying for this kind of thing and now you give it to me for nothing!" "Enter the city," said the wise man, "it is all yours." · H.C.

The ability to shift perspective—asking, "How can I see this differently?"—can be one of the most powerful and effective tools we have to help us cope with life's daily problems. · H.C.

IV.

Overcoming Obstacles

The first step in seeking happiness is learning—learning how the negative emotions and behaviors are harmful to us and how the positive emotions are helpful. . . . In bringing about positive changes within oneself, although learning is only the first step, there are other factors as well: conviction, determination, action, and effort. The next step is developing conviction.

Learning and education are important because they help one develop conviction of the need to change. This conviction to change then develops into determination. Next, one transforms determination into action—the strong determination to change enables one to make a sustained effort to implement the actual changes. This final factor of effort is critical.

Now, no matter what behavior you are seeking to change, no matter what particular goal or action you are directing your efforts toward, you need to start by developing a strong willingness or wish to do it. You need to generate great enthusiasm. And here, a sense of urgency is a key factor. This sense of urgency is a powerful factor in helping you overcome problems.

❋

In order to generate a sense of urgency to
engage in spiritual practices, the
practitioner is reminded of our
impermanence, of death. . . . That
awareness of impermanence is
encouraged, so that when it is coupled
with our appreciation of the enormous
potential of our human existence, it will
give us a sense of urgency that we must
use every precious moment.

By making a steady effort, I think we
can overcome any form of negative
conditioning and make positive changes
in our lives. But you still need to realize
that genuine change doesn't happen
overnight.

There is no getting around these essential ingredients: determination, effort, and time. These are the real secrets to happiness. · H.C.

All "deluded" states of mind, all afflictive emotions and thoughts, are essentially distorted, in that they are rooted in misperceiving the actual reality of the situation. No matter how powerful, deep down these negative emotions have no valid foundation. They are based on ignorance. On the other hand, all the positive emotions or states of mind, such as love, compassion, insight, and so on, have a solid basis. When the mind is experiencing these positive states, there is no distortion.

Our positive states of mind can act as antidotes to our negative tendencies and delusory states of mind. . . . As you enhance the capacity of these antidotal factors, the greater their force, the more you will be able to reduce the force of the mental and emotional afflictions, the more you will be able to reduce the influences and effects of these things.

Some suggest that since negative
emotions are a "natural" part of our
mind, there is no way to really overcome
them. But that is wrong. For example, all
of us are born in an ignorant state, so
ignorance is also quite "natural." If we
leave ourselves in our natural state
without making an effort to learn, we
won't be able to dispel ignorance. But as
we grow, we can acquire knowledge and

dispel ignorance through education. Similarly, through proper training we can gradually reduce our negative emotions and increase positive states of mind such as love, compassion, and forgiveness.

The very fact that we can change our emotions and counteract negative thoughts by applying alternative ways of thinking lends support to the Dalai Lama's position that we can overcome our negative mental states through the application of the "antidotes," or the corresponding positive mental states. And when this fact is combined with recent scientific evidence that we can change the structure and function of the brain by cultivating new thoughts, then the idea that we can achieve happiness through training of the mind seems a very real possibility. · H.C.

Dealing with expectations is really a tricky issue. If you have excessive expectations without a proper foundation, then that usually leads to problems. On the other hand, without expectation and hope, without aspiration, there can be no progress. Some hope is essential. So finding the proper balance is not easy. One needs to judge each situation on the spot.

The essential nature of mind is pure.
It is based on the belief that the underlying basic subtle consciousness is
untainted by the negative emotions. Its
nature is pure, a state that is referred
to as the "mind of Clear Light."
That basic nature of the mind is also
called Buddha Nature. So, since
the negative emotions are not an intrinsic

part of this Buddha Nature, there is a
possibility to eliminate them and purify
the mind.

Hatred and anger are considered to be the greatest evils because they are the greatest obstacles to developing compassion and altruism, and they destroy one's virtue and calmness of mind.

The destructive effects of anger and hatred are well documented by the many scientific studies showing these emotions to be a significant cause of disease and premature death. . . . In fact, hostility is now considered to be a major risk factor in heart disease. Of course, one doesn't need scientific evidence of the destructive nature of these emotions to realize how they can cloud our judgment, cause feelings of extreme discomfort, or wreak havoc in our personal relationships. Our personal experience can tell us that. · H.C.

Usually, we don't bother much about anger or hatred, so it just comes. But once we develop a cautious attitude toward these emotions, that reluctant attitude itself can act as a preventative measure against anger or hatred.

Feelings of anger and hatred arise from a
mind that is troubled by dissatisfaction
and discontent. So you can prepare ahead
of time by constantly working toward
building inner contentment and
cultivating kindness and compassion.
This brings about a certain calmness of
mind that can help prevent anger from
arising in the first place.

We cannot overcome anger and hatred
simply by suppressing them. We need to
actively cultivate the antidotes to them:
patience and tolerance. . . . Someone who
gains victory over hatred and anger
through such an arduous process is
a true hero.

If you can learn to develop patience and
tolerance toward your enemies, then
everything else becomes much easier—
your compassion toward all others begins
to flow naturally.

Now there are many, many people in the
world, but relatively few with whom we
interact, and even fewer who cause us
problems. So when you come across such
a chance for practicing patience and
tolerance, you should treat it with
gratitude. It is rare. Just as having
unexpectedly found a treasure in your
own house, you should be happy and
grateful toward your enemy for providing

that precious opportunity. Because if you are ever to be successful in your practice of patience and tolerance, which are critical factors in counteracting negative emotions, it is due to the combination of your own efforts and also the opportunity provided by your enemy.

In fact, the enemy is the necessary condition for practicing patience. Without an enemy's action, there is no possibility for patience or tolerance to arise. Our friends do not ordinarily test us and provide the opportunity to cultivate patience; only our enemies do this. So from this standpoint we can consider our enemy as a great teacher, and revere him or her for giving us this precious opportunity to practice patience.

Since patience or tolerance comes from an ability to remain firm and steadfast and not be overwhelmed by the adverse situations or conditions that one faces, one should see tolerance or patience not as a sign of weakness or giving in, but rather as a sign of strength, coming from a deep ability to remain firm.

An end result or product of patience and tolerance is forgiveness. When you are truly patient and tolerant, then forgiveness comes naturally.

Feelings of grief and anxiety are natural responses to loss. But if you allow these feelings of loss and worry to persist, there's a danger: if these feelings are left unchecked, they can lead to a kind of self-absorption.

If you find yourself worrying too much, it may help to think of the other people who have similar or even worse tragedies. Once you realize that, then you no longer feel isolated, as if you have been single-pointedly picked out. That can offer you some kind of condolence.

If a difficult situation or problem is such
that it can be remedied, then there is no
need to worry. In other words, if there is
a solution or a way out of the difficulty,
then one needn't be overwhelmed by
it. . . . It is more sensible to spend the
energy focusing on the solution rather
than worrying about the problem.
Alternatively, if there is no way out, no
solution, no possibility of resolution,

then there is also no point in worrying about it—because you can't do anything about it anyway.

In the Dalai Lama's system of training the mind and achieving happiness, the closer one gets to being motivated by altruism, the more fearless one becomes in the face of even extremely anxiety-provoking circumstances. · H.C.

Motivation is so important. In fact all human action can be seen in terms of movement, and the mover behind all actions is one's motivation. If you develop a pure and sincere motivation, if you are motivated by a wish to help on the basis of kindness, compassion, and respect, then you can carry on any kind of work, in any field, and function more effectively with less fear or worry, not

being afraid of what others think or
whether you ultimately will be successful
in reaching your goal.

I've found that sincere motivation acts as
an antidote to reduce fear and anxiety.

When looking at our underlying sense of "self," I think one can characterize two types. One sense of self, or "ego," is concerned only with the fulfillment of one's self-interest, one's selfish desires, with complete disregard for the well-being of others. The other type of ego or sense of self is based on a genuine concern for others and the desire to be of service. In order to fulfill that wish to be of service, one needs a strong sense of self, and a sense of self-confidence. This kind of self-confidence is the kind that leads to positive consequences.

The more honest you are, the more open, the less fear you will have, because there's no anxiety about being exposed or revealed to others. So, I think that the more honest you are, the more self-confident you will be.

It seems that when problems arise, our outlook often becomes narrow. All of our attention may be focused on worrying about the problem, feeling as if we're the only one going through such difficulties, which makes the problem seem very intense. When this happens, I think that shifting perspective, seeing things from a wider perspective, can definitely help. . . . If you only look at that one event, it appears bigger and bigger. If you focus too closely, too intensely, on a problem, it appears uncontrollable. But if you compare that situation with some other greater event, look at your problem from a different perspective, from a distance, then it appears smaller and less overwhelming.

V.

On Living a
Spiritual Life

We often hear people say that all human
beings are equal. By this we mean that
everyone has the obvious desire of
happiness. Everybody has the right to
be a happy person. And everyone has
the right to overcome suffering. So if
someone is deriving happiness or benefit
from a particular religious tradition, it
becomes important to respect the rights

of others; thus we must learn to respect all these major religious traditions. That is clear.

One way of strengthening mutual respect
between those of different religious
faiths is through closer contact. Personal
contact. Through this kind of closer
contact we can learn about the useful
contributions that these religions have
made to humanity, the positive things,
so when confronted with another
religion, initially a positive feeling, a
comfortable feeling, will arise. We'll feel

if that person finds a different tradition more suitable, more effective, then that's good! Then it's like going to a restaurant—we can all sit down at one table and order different dishes according to one's own taste—we might eat different dishes, but nobody argues about it!

There are so many things that divide humanity, so many problems in the world. Religion should be a remedy to help reduce the conflict and suffering in the world—not another source of conflict.

There can be two levels of spirituality.
One has to do with our religious beliefs.
If we believe in any religion, that's good.
But even without a religious belief, we
can still manage. In some cases, we can
manage even better. But that's our own
individual right; if we wish to believe,
good! If not, it's all right. But then
there's another level of spirituality. That
is what I call basic spirituality—basic

human qualities of goodness, kindness, compassion, caring. Whether we are believers or non-believers, this kind of spirituality is essential. I personally consider this second level of spirituality to be more important than the first, because no matter how wonderful a particular religion may be, it will still only be accepted by a limited number of human beings, only a portion of humanity. But as long as we are human beings, as long as we are members of the human family, all of us need these basic spiritual values. Without these, human existence remains hard, very dry. As a result, none of us can be a happy person, our whole family will suffer, and then, eventually, society will be more troubled. So, it becomes clear that cultivating these kinds of basic spiritual values becomes crucial.

If you understand spiritual practice in its true sense, then you can use all twenty-four hours of your day for your practice. True spirituality is a mental attitude that you can practice at any time.

Real spiritual practice is in some sense like a voltage stabilizer. The function of the stabilizer is to prevent irregular power surges and instead give you a stable and constant source of power.

Engaging in training or a method of bringing about inner discipline within one's mind is the essence of a religious life, an inner discipline that has the purpose of cultivating these positive mental states. Thus, whether one leads a spiritual life depends on whether one has been successful in bringing about that disciplined, tamed state of mind and translating that state of mind into one's

daily actions.

Investigators have found that even an artifi-

cially induced frown or smile tends to induce the

corresponding emotions of anger or happiness; this

suggests that just "going through the motions"

and repeatedly engaging in a positive behavior

can eventually bring about genuine internal

change. · H.C.

Although one's experiences are a
consequence of one's past deeds, that
does not mean that the individual has no
choice or that there is no room for
initiative to change. . . . One should not
become passive and try to excuse oneself
from having to take personal initiative on
the grounds that everything is a result
of Karma, because if one understands
the concept of Karma properly, one

will understand that Karma means "action." . . . So what type of future will come about, to a large extent, lies within our own hands in the present. It will be determined by the kinds of initiatives that we take now.

Now the secret to my own happiness,
my own good future, is within my own
hands. I must not miss that opportunity!

ABOUT THE AUTHORS

HIS HOLINESS THE DALAI LAMA was born on July 6, 1935, to a poor farming family in northeastern Tibet. At the age of two he was recognized as the Dalai Lama, the spiritual and temporal leader of Tibet, the fourteenth in a succession dating back six hundred years. At age six he began his lifelong training as a Buddhist monk. Since 1959, he has lived in exile from Tibet in Dharamsala, India. His tireless efforts on behalf of human rights, world peace, and basic human values have brought him international recognition. He is the recipient of numerous honors and awards, among them the 1989 Nobel Peace Prize and a U.S. Congressional Gold Medal.

For more information about the Dalai Lama, including his schedule of teachings, please visit www.dalailama.com.

HOWARD C. CUTLER, M.D., is a psychiatrist, best-selling author, and speaker. He is coauthor, with His Holiness the Dalai Lama, of the acclaimed Art of Happiness series of books, which have been translated into fifty languages and have appeared on bestseller lists around the world. As a leading expert on the science of human happiness and a pioneer in the field of positive psychology, Dr. Cutler gives keynote presentations, leads workshops, and teaches courses on happiness throughout the world.

He is a diplomate of the American Board of Psychiatry and Neurology and is on the editorial board of the *American Journal of Psychotherapy*. Dr. Cutler has dedicated his life to helping others find greater happiness, fulfillment, and success. He lives in Phoenix.

For more information about *The Art of Happiness*, including books, workshops, and courses, or to contact Dr. Cutler, visit www.theartofhappiness.com.